Migrant Sun

Miscellanea

Migrant Sun

Ramón Ledesma

© 2013 by Ramon Ledesma

ISBN Number: 978-0-615-75653-0

Library of Congress Control Number: 2013930953

Published by Migrant Sun Press

Printed by Village Books on the Espresso Book Machine
in the United States of America

Available at Village Books, Bellingham WA
www.villagebooks.com   360-671-2626

Cover art by Jess Arashi Hara

Migrant Sun is dedicated to my papá, Juan, a tough man who taught me the virtues of perseverance and hard work and to my mamá, Rosa, a loving woman who filled my imagination with prophetic images of the wonderful things that come to those who believe.

Poems

Your Fields

We've walked to your fields at dawn.
We labored in the noon-day sun.
We returned, spent from your fields at dusk.
We are a million browns
In the migrant fields,
At harvest time in America.

We've picked your tomatoes, cucumbers and lettuce.
We've picked your apples, peaches and oranges.
We've eaten the dust of a thousand tractors;
The dust settling on us in delicate layers
Until our pesticide sweat
Ran like a burning yellow river
Down the valley of our backs.

We've lain in rat infested shacks
In winter so cold our brothers and sisters
Froze dead in their sleep.
We buried them on the outskirts
Of your cemeteries;
Too poor to buy them markers.
We can no longer find them
Anywhere, but in the troubled
Darkness of our nightmares.

We've come to your hospitals—in desperation,
Pleading for healing of our young.
We've placed them on your sterile altars—
examination tables,
Only to watch them die from neglect,
In hidden, taupe colored rooms—alone.
They died waiting for the nurses to call,
And doctors who never showed,
Who never cared,
About the poor, brown,
Children who waited,
And suffered;

To die like dogs,
Abandoned
By the side of the road.
Our young,
    A thousand,
        More or less grow cold.

        Your fields.

Mamá Dreamed Of Flowers

Mamá dreamed of flowers;
Sweet scented petals
To take away the pungent
Smell of the day's sweat
And add color to a weary,
Punishing, unforgiving life
Between the dusty rows
And the migrant's death echoes.

Mamá dreamed of
Carnations and Heather,
Lilacs and Queen Anne's Lace,
To grow in the withering,
Vacant places in her heart,
Left by empty promises
From hardened, brown men
Battered, bruised and humiliated
By a migrant's life.

Mamá dreamed of love
But when it came
It was a robin's song:
Short, intense and sweet.
Mamá dreamed of a lasting love.
Mama's dreams have lasted,
But her loves, she's buried.

Papá knew nothing of love.
He had little to share.
He was born in the lust
Of whiskey
And raised in bile of
A scoundrel's fate.

Mamá dreamed of children.
The only promise Papá kept;
The only honesty
Papá knew.

Mamá wanted children,
Not just one
Or maybe two,
She needed many to
Receive her love,
To share her dreams.
Her children were her flowers.

Mamá dreamed of dancing
In crimson lace,
In courtly halls,
In all her grace.

Mamá dreamed of traveling
In trains and planes
To beautiful cities:
France and Spain.

Mamá dreamed of houses,
Cars and midnight stars,
With colorful, silk scarves
From foreign bazaars.

Mamá dreamed of watching
Her children grow strong,
Being successful,
Where they belonged.

Mamá dreamed about forever,
Neither here nor there
But in our hearts;
A love affair.

Mamá dreamed of flowers.

Linoleum Floor

Faded, worn linoleum floor,
Patterns now obscured
And lost forevermore;
Where labored feet once tread
Now detoured,
Their spirits grace instead.

Mamá stood by kitchen sink
Washed the dishes clean,
Mesmerized by her dreams.
As she gazed out the window
She hummed a soft Mexican song
While she watched her children playing
In the dirt courtyard.

Papá sat by wood stove
And rocked in the evening.
Cigar smoke bellowed white
Above his head
And parallel grooves he wore,
Like train tracks in the floor.

Those whom time too soon betrayed
Show no fear;
They linger still among us,
Weighty then,
More gently now.

No longer do they pass,
Yet, when the sun takes rest
Behind the mountain mass,
And I lie down—I do attest;
I hear their thoughts
And glance ethereal forms.
They will remain as guests.

Faded, worn linoleum floor.

The Sacrifice

I've been awakened in dark by whispers.
I've been awakened in dark by anger.
I've eaten breakfast under a single,
Lonely, dangling, incandescent bulb,
In a dilapidated migrant laborer's shack;
The bruja's threatening shadow
Dancing malevolently on the wall,
Listening for the call—
Waiting for my fall—

I've labored in fields of rain,
My blood flowed murky and dark—like the rain
Down the sugar beet rows.
I've labored in fields set ablaze by the blistering sun.
Hell attempted to claim my soul.

I've labored in fields frozen white with early snow.
My feet have frozen, but I didn't complain.
I've cut off my own fingers and not felt the pain.
I've labored in fields with my brothers and sisters.
Side by side—we worked,
Our nubile bodies sacrificed and spent.
We were there, but no one noticed.
We were there, but no one cared.

The sacrifice.

Winters, Like Papá

Winters, like Papá,
Were harsh and cruel.
We fed the stove with coal fuel.

Working frozen fields by day,
And on winter nights we hid
Beneath Mamá's thick quilts,
Made from worn-out blankets
And tattered clothes—with love.

Mamá's quilts protected us—from the chill
That ate our toes, noses and elbows
On those cold, sunless mornings...
But not from Papá's will.

Winters, like Papá,
Were harsh and cruel.
We fed the stove with coal fuel.

Frail and vulnerable we lay—under warm quilts
When he entered
He separated us from sleep,
And all there was to keep us warm,
Announcing day's work:
Milk the cows
Feed the pigs
Keep the rust from tractor rig.

Tears and quiet sobs,
Fearful gulps, silent terror.

As a child there is so much
A heart does not understand,
So much it fears;
The bitter cold, the dark,
The frozen fields,
The man with the iron will
That foist them all upon us.

Winters, like Papá
Were harsh and cruel
We fed the fire with coal fuel.

I feared his thick, callused hands,
His animal steely stare
And unreasonable demands.
As a child you learn that
Life is lived
At harsh command.

I hated the cold, its icy chill,
The frozen ground,
His rigid stiff-necked will.

I feared his presence
And those frigid mornings
And with every uncaring hand
He lay on my frail
Body, I learned to hate
Him as well.

Tears and quiet sobs,
Fearful gulps, silent terror.

Winters, like Papá,
Were harsh and cruel
We fed the stove with coal fuel.

Winters, like Papá.

Water

The clear, glass gallon
Water jug lies half buried
In the brown dirt,
At the end of the row.
It's a long way to go,
And progress is slow.

I straighten my bent back
And turn to look.
I squint,
To gauge the distance,
But the sun has affected my sight.
Not quite right.

My depth perception
Is distorted.
I look down the long row
Of sugar beets.
My vision narrows.

It seems like a mile
It will be a good long while.

I feel suddenly disoriented.
I try to swallow;
Nothing but dust.
I cough
And choke.

I grab the long handled hoe
In both hands;
Left in front of right.
I lift it a few feet
And bring it down
On the weeds,
Pull it back

And up—towards me.
It's a clumsy motion
I've done a thousand times today.
I step to my right.

It seems like a mile.
It will be a good long while.

Over and over again
I'll repeat the clumsy motion
Until I reach the end
Of the row.

Water.

Tin Roofs And Rainy Days

In that tenuous space between wake and dreams, I listened to the syncopated sounds of raindrops playing Requiem for a Migrant Child, solemnly on the corrugated tin roof above my head. Resisting wakefulness, I struggled to keep the cold, damp morning air out and warmth and comfort of sleep in. We were living in a labor camp outside Sedro-Woolley, Washington. Summer had begun. But in the Pacific Northwest, a June rain can be indistinguishable from a cold and miserable November.

As wakefulness overcame sleep, my mind became cognizant. The patter of rain began to play a different tune: one as sweet as a Beethoven sonata. Rain meant work would be postponed! On rainy days the fertile brown soil between the rows was soaked, and when trodden on, quickly became muddied and impassable. Work would have to wait until the sun dried out the rows. If we were lucky, we could snatch a couple more hours of sleep, and still reclaim half day away from the arduous fields of labor that consumed our young lives.

I smiled to myself and burrowed deeper under the thick quilt Mamá had made to keep us warm. Even a few extra minutes beneath it brought comfort to my heart. Having so little time to be a child, I relished every minute away from the fields.

Most Anglo children have no concept of free time, just as fish have no concept of water. For them, free time is the very definition of childhood. Not so with Mexican migrant children who are in the fields working as soon as they can maneuver a long-handled hoe. To us, those rain-washed, free-time days were a blessing and a joy.

Beneath Mamá's quilt, my mind digressed to a perplexing experience from the past. My mind wandered back to a hot day in a field not far from camp.

The blistering heat had been slowly cooking another layer of dust and sweat on any surface exposed to the sun. Across the field I had watched the farmer's children joyfully playing on a luscious green lawn around their beautiful, three-story, Victorian home. The sprinkler had been spraying cool water on the lawn and the children were running in and out of it, screaming with delight. I had struggled to understand why some children played and others like me, and my brothers and sisters, worked. Yes, we had our moments of play, but those were short-lived, and punctuated by long stretches of hard labor, usually under unforgiving weather conditions. For us, play was an anomaly, not the definition of childhood, as it was with the farmer's children.

Why didn't they have to work the fields their parents owned, I had wondered. After all, the fields belonged to them. And why couldn't I have been playing with them on the green lawns? And finally, I had compared the lush green lawns and beautiful home to the dilapidated shacks, unfit as pig shelter, we lived in. These questions I had pondered as I worked.

A dirt clod had exploded on my bony chest. I had looked up to see my brothers laughing at me. I had gotten the message and had quickly turned my attention back to picking.

But I could not reconcile the images in my mind. I had languished behind the others, struggling with the incongruities of life while my siblings feverishly worked on. So I made a mental note and filed that day under, "Ask Mamá why." I knew I had work to do, and if I didn't get back to it, the next dirt clod might have a rock in it. So I had gone back to picking, one in the basket, two in the mouth with my usual unproductivity trickling red down my chin.

From under the warmth of covers, the conundrum ran through my mind as I contemplated the cold woodstove. The fire was long out. I lay there, wondering, as I uncovered my head enough to gaze sheepishly around the small cold shack I shared with four brothers. I saw lumps but no heads, feet, or arms. Like me, they were too cold to expose themselves to the morning chill. Each of us, I knew, was either waiting for someone else to get up and rekindle a fire from the cold gray ashes, or just engaged in the neverland of dreams that compensated for the deficiencies of our real life. I wondered what they were dreaming. Thinking it an older brother's duty, I retreated further into my cocoon. Juan was usually the one. He had always been the responsible one, and could be counted on to do the right thing. Within a few minutes I heard stirrings. I peeked out from under the covers. Sure enough, it was Juan. I loved Juan, God's answer to my prayer, despite my slothfulness.

In the periphery of my consciousness lingered the smell of breakfast cooking in the next cabin. The wonderful scents found their way through the holes in the decaying walls and tested my resolve to stay under the covers a little longer. The longer I stayed in my world of dreams, the less breakfast would be left to enjoy. In our family, he who woke late for breakfast would certainly be the first to lunch.

The fire, snapping and crackling, was beginning to warm the cold cabin air as I rose and quietly put my clothes on. Juan was back in bed, so all I saw was lumps under covers. Outside, I could hear the camp foreman making his rounds, knocking on cabin doors telling everyone the day's work would be delayed until after the rain. He was our town crier. I opened the door, quickly stepped outside and closed it behind me. Standing under the short eaves of the tin roof, I contemplated stepping into the now hard-falling rain. The raindrops were big as northwest strawberries. I looked through the falling drops to my destination and calculated how wet I was going to be when I reached it and how cold I was getting remaining where I was. I surmised it would take a Jesse-Owens, Olympic-caliber sprint to stay dry and indecision wasn't getting me any warmer. Without warning, my brain sent the message to my legs and I found myself leaping off the top step and straight into a puddle. Not my best jump. As I hit the puddle, water splashed high into the air but not a drop landed on me as I sprinted like I was shot out of a cannon. I made it to Mamá's cabin in less than three seconds. It had to have been a camp record. As I tagged the door I turned in time to see the water in the swirling air currents created by the turbulence of my lightning speed. I heard thunder and wondered if it was my sonic boom. I was dry as a piece of kindling beside a hot woodstove on a summer's day.

I sat for a few minutes watching Mamá and the girls, Raquel and Dolores, preparing breakfast. There was a small lump in the top bunk. Linda. She was a late riser. Juan was the next to enter the cabin. Then Enrique followed by Mario and Arturo. It wasn't long before we heard the foreman's knock. Eight heads turned in unison to hear the morning's news. Mamá kept her focus on the meal she was preparing, but her ears registered the knock—and the message. "Work will be delayed at least a half day!" he yelled. Mama cringed; the rest of us smiled. For obvious reasons, Mamá did not like rainy days: they meant loss of wages. Loss of wages meant less food. Rainy days were serious business to Mamá. Not that she grumbled. Mamá was not a complainer. But the news affected the lines on her face.

"After breakfast and before you leave, I have some chores that need to be done," Mamá said, getting back to the tortillas on the hot stove. My brothers and I were instructed to replenish the cabin's wood supply so my sisters could dry the laundry they had to wash by hand in another part of the camp. Juan and Enrique chopped the wood; Mario and I helped carry it into the cabin. Arturo, being too young for any kind of work, just followed us back and forth like a puppy dog.

After the clothes were washed and hung inside on cords stretched between the cabin walls, the girls fed the fire while Mamá inquired with the other mothers in the camp if any were going into town. She wanted to catch a ride to buy groceries and run errands. One or both of the girls always went with her because she could neither read nor write English. None of us boys wanted to go; we considered it "women's work." And if we did go, it was to run the streets, not to help Mamá. Accordingly, once the fires were going,

Mamá had turned us loose to do as we pleased, with the stipulation we returned by lunch.

My brothers and I roamed the camp, gathering friends to help plan a few hours of fun. In the rain we ran through the woods like prisoners freed from solitary confinement. There were dense, wet woods, deep and mysterious, to explore; old barns full of abandoned machinery and furniture; haylofts full of dried-out hay to play in. We flew jets, invaded evil empires, fought in jungles, invented life-saving medicines, and saved civilization from evil. In small groups we ran through the pastures, woods, and barns, unwrapping the rainy day like a beautiful Christmas gift. For a few short hours we were allowed to be children.

Having little was sometimes not the liability in youth that it could be in adulthood. As I look back from a different culture, from a more affluent and plentiful period, I realize that the poverty of youth had been fertile fields, rich in imagination and limitless creativity. I came to realize, having little might have been less a burden and more of a blessing.

I placed a high value on my free time. Those short times of play were a precious commodity that encouraged me to live more passionately. And in part, although I didn't recognize it then, watching the farmer's children's joyful play did not only create confusion and resentment. That initially painful exposure also spawned hope for what the future might possibly hold for us. But the concepts of hope and future were not easy to embrace with the sun hot on your head and sweat running down the small of your aching back.

Then add into the equation the danger of our lifestyle. Living took on greater urgency. If our past taught us anything, it was that not even the present, poor as it might have been, is certain—much less a future rich with plenty.

As a child I didn't realize the affect losing four of our older siblings had on our young psyches. To us, death was not an abstraction. It was as real as the rain that soaked and sun that scorched us. Yes, death had always been on our minds.

It wasn't until we successfully reached adulthood that we were able to admit it. After the death of our oldest sister, Maria, Enrique and I went to a tavern to anesthetize our grief and raw emotions with beer. He confided he had always wondered if he would be the fifth of our parents' children to die. I started. As a child, I'd had the same dark thought, the same deep-seated fear.

Hope for our future was the fuel that drove us to get up every morning and work till the sun set, hoping that our hard work would result in a better, more meaningful and perhaps a safer life. Nevertheless, often when the sun was scorching and the day in the fields too long, our hope faded. Fearing we would give up, Mamá gave us her dreams.

Mamá's dreams were like diamonds—clear and bright. She was careful that they not be taken by evil winds or robbed by jealous spirits: she shared them with us in hushed tones and gentle whispers. She knew if she could teach us to dream, we could hope. From that, she somehow believed we could create a future in which we could succeed. Where her hope came from was, for years, a mystery to me. This was a woman not afforded the love and attention in her youth, that she showered on us as children. From a young age she was made to work in harsher conditions than ours. Her life was more akin to slavery and never had the luxury of the umbrella of hope and dreams she sheltered and nurtured us under. The final curse? She saw four of her children die in front of her.

Where in God's name did her hope come from? Being intimately aware of the dangers we confronted in our daily lives, where did she get the courage to dream and find the strength to share those dreams with us? I asked her that very question not too long ago and her answer surprised me. With tears filling her eyes, she raised her proud head and simply said, "From my children." We gave her hope and in turn she gifted us with a more powerful hope in return.

As we worked the fields, or ate bean burritos in the shade of towering fir trees, she spoke to us in her mesmerizing, melodic Spanish voice, assuring us her dreams of our future were real. In spite all we'd been through, she considered it a victory that we were together. And now with her dreams embedded in our minds and her hope emblazoned in our hearts, she was sure the Promised Land was just over the hill and around the bend. If we believed, were patient, and worked hard, it was ours for the earning. And she assured us it would all come to be, far from the filth of the camps we lived in, far from the pesticide-laced crops we worked in. And far from el patron, who made his living with his boot on our necks and his greedy hand in our pockets.

And she was right.

There isn't a day that goes by that I don't judge where I am and what I have by the standard of our beginnings …and deem it all beautiful.

The Soil Of A Thousand Farms

The soil of a thousand farms
I see in dreams' alarm.
The soil so dark and rich
Watered by the salty sweat
Of a million brown brows.

The soil of a thousand farms
Is irrigated from ditches
That run crimson with the blood
Of my brothers and sisters.

On the soil of a thousand farms
We lost an innocence
That once glowed white
That once was bright.
But now lies fallow
With the stench of
Echoes hollow.

The soil of a thousand farms.

The Photograph

There they are,
Hanging on the wall—three;
Calmly,
Serenely looking across the room
In photograph
Of black and white.

Beautiful faces,
With haunting eyes,
Are children's graces,
In hard times.

Mischievous Enrique—
In Davy Crockett tee,
Bear and musket on his chest,
The lone wolf was his crest.
A troubled life manifest,
Unlike the rest.

Handsome Juan—
In bright shirt white,
Rabbit's foot on his belt.
He was everyone's delight,
For family honor,
And you and me, he'd fight.

And Ramón, insecure
And sad,
In striped tee,
Belt buckle to the right,
Bracelet on his wrist,
Arm resting on Juan's shoulder.
Standing above the rest
But would never stand
The test.

Somber gazes
From thoughtful faces.
The hard life in their eyes,
A migrant's way,
No need to apologize.

A firm resolve,
There to evolve,
Their own separate ways;
Enrique, a life of tough rebelliousness,
Juan the rock,
Steady and calm,
And Ramón the seer.
Who could read your fortune,
Didn't need your palm,
Fortune cookies or crystal ball.
He found it all there,
In your face.
It's no disgrace.
A childhood gift.
From inner space.

The photograph
Was taken at
The Cherry Blossom Festival,
In Sunnyside,
The Washington one.
Mamá wanted them
Together.
She was proud of them.
She loved the picture.
She loved her children.

The photograph.

The Ghost

He is the frail, brown skinned boy
With dirty elbows
Twice hand-me-down jeans
And stained, faded tee shirt
Sitting on the splintered wooden steps
Of the rat infested migrant shack
Ten miles out of town.
He won't be there long,
Long enough to let sadness
Sink deep—take root;
Impoverish innocence
Until he wears the sadness
Like his dirty brown skin.
Both will follow him
Through a hard life
To an early grave.

But it's not the rat-infested shack
That sits on the river bank
Where he lives
    When the leaves
    Are green and lush
    And the fruit is ripe,
Across the valley from the
Victorian mansions
And white picket fences
That impoverishes his soul.

It's not the hopelessness
That covers him like
A heavy quilt
When the sun goes down
And the work is done
That impoverishes his soul.

It's not poverty's
Dark shadow that
Haunts his footsteps
Away from the fields
And into the classroom
That impoverishes his soul.

It's the dismissive teacher
That seats him in the back,
Separating him from the
Dial-soap scented,
Pallid skinned children,
Where he wonders why he's alone;
Why he's looking
At their backs,
That impoverishes his soul.

It's the haughty eyes
That gaze with distain
As he quietly sits...
Dirty hands folded in his lap
Patiently waiting to understand,
Patiently waiting to learn,
That impoverishes his soul.

It's condescending smirks
On colorless children's faces
Condemning him
Rejecting him.
Singularly he stands on the playground
Waiting for a ball
That is never kicked his way
That impoverish his soul.

It's the God-fearing, self righteous
Parents that teach their children
That they and only they
Are good and know the Christian way
That impoverishes his soul.

His ghost has sat on a thousand wooden steps
In a thousand poverty shacks
In a thousand agricultural communities
When the migrant sun was high
And warm on the fields.

His ghost has worked from
Sunup to sundown
In the fields
Where the pesticide mist
Mixed with fine dust
Filled the heavy humid air
In his lungs and circulated poison
Through his body.

His ghost sits and watches
The other world
Pass by as if
He didn't exist.
A ghost in the land of
Promise and opportunity.

The dirty brown boy is a ghost
And that is what impoverishes his soul.

The Ghost.

The Dirt Beneath My Feet

The dirt beneath my feet is my soul.
I walk barefoot alone
Through dark, chocolate dirt
In fields lain fallow.
Soil soft—scented of a young boy's dreams,
Childhood schemes and unrequited prayers.

But dreams and prayers
Like late summer fruit, once ripe with hope
Now brown—lays rot;
Drowned in salty tears
Of an old man's laments,
And life's regrets.

Dreams and prayers
And mindful schemes;
Of young and old
For naught it seems.

Skin—dry, taut and opaque,
Weak eyes of old, too dim to see
And bones too frail for work.
The labor of life's absurdity.

The dirt beneath my feet is my soul.

Sunday Windows

Papá drove us to town
And parked on the
Edge of Paradise,
On the bank of the Skagit River.

The windows...
They waited for us there,
On those beautiful
Sunday afternoons,
Away from the fields.

The opaque images
Reflected mother and child,
Hand in hand,
As we moved slowly
From one store front
Window to another.

Mamá looked at brightly
Colored flowered dresses,
For balmy, summer evening
Dances in the courtyard
And picnic bonnets for walks
Along the cool river bank.

I looked at red Radio Flyers
To race down dusty roads,
And Yankees baseball caps
To keep the sun out of my eyes
When running for fly-balls
In pitted pastures.

Mama's soft Spanish voice
Whispered the mysteries
Of the storefront
Windows to me.

I pointed to my
Tee-shirt reflection...
"There goes Davy Crockett," I said,
 And Mamá laughed.

From one end of town to the other,
We walked,
Gazed,
Pointed,
And frequently stopped
To inspect the contents
Of the storefront windows.

We laughed,
Held hands,
Whispered,
And told secrets.

We had no money,
But none was needed.
We owned the windows,
And the storefronts,

The baseball caps,
Brightly colored,
Flowered dresses,
Picnic bonnets,
And Radio Flyers.

On Sundays, we owned
Paradise.

Sunday windows.

Sixth Of July

Fourth Street;
Toppenish town,
Corner house,
With the elm tree
And the henhouse.

Hot July, mid-day sun;
Bloody water splashed
On faded, linoleum floor,
Nothing to ignore,
Says it's time for sure.

Run down the street mijo
Tell la Señora Rodríguez—
The midwife,
It's time to come
Get her on the run.

Lie down Mamá
Oh, mija, I don't want to complain
But here comes the pain.
Mija, get the clean rags
Mamá set aside last week.
They're in the brown bag.
And draw the water
From the well,
Hurry, this child will come,
On the pain, I can not dwell.

Oh, my—Señora
It's another boy
Don't you have
Five of those already, Rosa?
Oh, yes I do
But one more,
Will have to do.

Sixth of July.

On The Edge Of Town

I walked the sun-scorched
Windswept fields
On the edge of town.

Lost in the wind,
Obscured by the dust
Swirling in a whirlwind
My feet kicked up
As I shuffled along the row,
Hoe in hand.

My clothes were dirty.
My hands callused and hard.
With every breath I took
The dust I breathed.
With every swallow,
The dirt I ate
Until it clogged my pores
And rendered me claustrophobic
Within myself.

From the soil I came
To wander earth
To the soil I'll go
And mourn my birth.

I washed the dirt
That clogged my spirit,
With the rain water
Running over the hardened
Ground surfaces:
Falling from the tin roofs
Of the dilapidated shacks I
Awoke in—
Praying, momentarily I was
Somewhere far away
From where I was.

When I knew,
When I saw—
Something died.
I understood—

I had no recourse,
No other place to be.
No one wanted me.

From the soil I came
To wander earth
To the soil I'll go
And mourn my birth.

I suffered silently
The indignities
You spat at me;
The glares you shot at me
When I dared get
Too close.

I screamed within,
But you couldn't hear.
I cried without,
But you didn't see.
How could you know?
But maybe you could,
Had you wanted to,
But you didn't,
And never would.

I bowed my head
And turned around
My very nature
You cut down.

Your violence, my flesh it ate.
Your damnations I consumed
Like pesticide water.
The sun burned me
And the wind took my breath away,
But still I stayed.

From the soil I came
To wander earth
To the soil I'll go
And mourn my birth.

I walked the sun-scorched
Windswept fields
On the edge of town.

My Brother's Clothes

I'm walking in my brother's clothes.
There are patches where once were holes.
I'm watching cars pass by.
A life that's empty, I can't deny.

I'm walking in my brother's shoes.
The more I walk the more the blues.
I'm looking into people's eyes.
They blink, frown, and then they sigh.

I carry with me my brother's fears.
My burdened heart is their souvenir.
If life is about fear and love,
Is fear below and love above?

I wear the scars of a million browns
Who've been kicked, spat and beaten down.
Stop us, try—you never will.
If the river is closed, then up the hill.

Pass your laws, stamp your bills.
We'll mate with fate and not be stilled.
Your minutemen will come and go.
Aqua sucia then Bordeaux.

I'm walking in my brother's clothes.

Muerte

I saw death coming
From across the street.

Man drunk
With a rifle—22 it was,
Small but violent.
Small but deadly.
Pop—it said,
And nothing more,
What more could there be
In the unsteady hands
Of the death maker.

Sister swinging—
Laughing.
Mamá pushing—
Smiling,
Watching her beautiful girl
Flying high—
Then return.
Mamá pushing—
Smiling
Flying high...
Pop—
Then she dropped—
Hard,
Sister did...
To the ground
With small red hole
In infant, innocent chest.
Sister down in Toppenish Town.

I saw death coming
From across the street.

Migrant Sun

Humped back,
Stooped shoulders,
We shuffled along
Row after row,
Hour after hour,
In the hot migrant sun.

Bent backs
And listless spirits;
We moved
Like strange alien beings,
Silent aberrations upon
A fertile land,
In the hot migrant sun.

We walked along dusty rows,
As in a trance,
A slow and easy cadence,
An eerie migrant dance
Upon the land,
In the hot migrant sun.

The fields our prisons,
The rows our cells,
In solitary confinement—we moved.
Eternity and the glass water jug
Lay buried at the end of the row,
In the hot migrant sun.

Don't look son,
Papá warned,
Across those acres.
Don't do it!
The rows—they will meet you,
One by one,
But, the acres will defeat you.
No way to win,
In the hot migrant sun.

Angry eyes
Sunburned lips
Parched throats.
How will I make it,
How will I last,
Across the dusty valley,
In the hot migrant sun?

Migrant sun.

Mamá Knew

What was she thinking,
As she watched them
Laboring in the fields,
Playing in the courtyard;
Her young, strong children,
Deeply tanned
From living with the sun?

They had big expansive eyes
That danced and laughed,
And shy smiles
That charmed you.

If you were careful, patient,
You could catch her
Watching them
With her heart
In her eyes.
And at that moment
They exploded with the light
Of a hundred suns.
They were clear and bright.

At other times,
If you looked—just right,
You could see
The dark menacing clouds
Above a great sadness,
So forbidden and disturbing
You had to break your gaze.
You had to look away.

It was the pain
Of a million mourners;
The grieving collective
Of migrant mamás,
Because they knew.
And Mamá too.

54

Yes...this America
Was their new life.
A life of unimaginable freedom
And opportunity.
But it wasn't free,
Of that she could see.
And she didn't trust this
American happiness
A migrant lives,
As she watched her children play.
She knew it had a price
And it ran the color of
Her deeply tanned children's
    Blood.

She knew there
Was a price to pay.
And it would
    Be paid,
        In full.

She knew its putrid smell.
She knew its bitter taste.
It felt like
The darkest night
In the deepest hell.
It had come before.
It would come again.

Mamá knew.

Last Night

Last night I dreamed I was free.
I saw myself walking the fertile fields
And roaming the Horse Heaven Hills,
That are my backyard.

Last night I was free.
I ran with the jackrabbits.
I jumped and zigzagged
Through the sagebrush,
Disappearing into the wild
And blazing sun.

Last night I was free.
I was a prairie dog
Peeking my head out of my home,
Chattering noisily to my neighbors.

Last night I was free.
I was the hawk
Flying high above the hills,
Riding the warm air currents
Looking for a meal.

Last night I was free.
I saw myself,
I was the cool water
In the irrigation canal above the fields.
I flowed freely
To the orchards and through the fields.

Last night I was free,
But when I woke
I was lying on a flea-bitten mattress
In a dilapidated migrant worker's shack.
For a few moments
I listened to the patter of the rain
On the metal roof—in disbelief.
And then I cried.

My tears formed dirty pools
Of muddy, salty water on the filthy mattress.
I knew they were not mine alone,
But those of a million
Browns that would never be free.
My spirit fell like the rain
Falling all around.

Last night I dreamed I was free.

I've Felt Your Eyes

I've felt your eyes—glancing,
momentarily...
No need to linger.
Scorn and disgust
Written on your faces,
And in your eyes;
Dirty, unkempt child they said,
Return from whence you came,
Only heaven knows,
It's now time to go.

From the labor of the fields,
I've seen you hide your faces,
Behind serene and graceful places.
Long, white picket fences
And tall, stately, maple trees
Stood guard
Over your perfectly manicured, green lawns
And white, antiseptic lives.

From air conditioned rooms,
You peered out of
Clean, clear windows
(The eyes of your red, brick palaces).
And I've heard your voices—whispers really,
Condemn and curse
It could be worse, Papá said.
His song and verse.
I've seen your cars
In cement perfect driveways,
New, shining like the sun,
Sparkling like the stars
For your Sunday morning drives
To Christian churches painted white
Thanking Jesus, so polite.

And your swimming pools,
They hurt the most.
The cool, clear water,
And ice tea,
For me to see,
While I shuffled, hoe in hand,
Like water on the sand,
Invisible,
Row after row
Beneath the migrant sun.

I've felt your eyes.

It Was Long Ago

It was so long ago,
I'd almost forgotten when.
It was summer I think,
That came and went.

I was kneeling in the dirt of a strawberry field
On a misty morning glen.
I was lying on a flea-bitten mattress,
In a shack—I was eight years old.
I was alone.

I was running through the woods—the smell of pine
trees in my nose.
It was Sunday—it was fun-day.
I was walking hand in hand with Mamá.
Down First Street in Mount Vernon—a baseball mitt
reflecting in my eyes.

She was wearing a faded, flowery summer dress—she
was beautiful.
It was fall—and I was waiting for the call.
The message that would lead me;
My way out—of the nightmare I was in,
I saw no end.
It was then, mama touched me.
She was listening to my soul.

This isn't your world, mijo—I heard her whisper.
We're living in my world.
Your world is up ahead,
Around the corner
And up the bend.
You can see it from here—
Your world—if you look hard.
Look down that long potholed road, mijo.
It has twists and turns and some dead ends.
Look, see that red brick school building,

Not too far away?
See that beautiful white house,
A little further down the road?
Be patient—it's there.
And look at that—
A shiny red car just passed by!
My, oh mijo, did you see it all?

No Mamá I didn't see a thing!

It's because you're looking with your eyes, mijo.
To see it all, you have to look with your heart—
To see, you have to trust me.
You have to believe in me.
This is hope I'm giving you, mijo.

What is hope Mamá?

Hope is the road ahead, mijo.
Hope is the road you must travel.

When are we going Mamá?

No mijo, hope is a road one travels alone.
I can't come with you, this time.

No Mamá, no!
I can't make it on my own!
I'm too young.
I'm not strong like you, Mamá.
You need to show me the way—to keep me safe.

Sorry mijo, I traveled mine,
Now you must travel yours.

I'm scared Mamá—don't leave me!

You may be young, mijo,
But I made you strong—I'm sure of that.
Because—
I've fed you on my dreams,
And nourished you with my stories.
I've put the future in your heart,
And clothed you with my strength.
You can do it, mijo. I believe in you.
But this is as far as I can take you.
The rest of the journey is yours.
But remember as you make your way.
And have children of your own.
When your journey's finished,
It's your responsibility
To show them the way,
To feed them on your dreams
And nourish them with your stories.
Put the future in their hearts,
And clothe them with your strength, mijo.
And when they're ready—
Take them by the hand,
And show them to the road.
Point the way—and push them on.
Like a mama robin with her chicks,
In the trees—high above the ground.
When they're ready—
She pushes them out of the nest,
Then watches them fall,
Catch a current and fly away.
It breaks her heart to do that,
Like mine is breaking now—to push you,
And to let you go.
But I have to, mijo.

I'm afraid Mamá!

Sí, mijo, so am I,
But remember—
Fear is what drives us,
Hope is what guides us.

It was long ago.

The Farmer's Walk

Why Papá called—
On those warm summer days,
I'll never know.
He gave no reason why,
It was his way.
And I didn't ask.

I'd stop what I was doing,
And ask no questions why.
From where I stood
I'd come running,
To his side and together
Walk, the farmer's walk.

"Let's check the irrigation," was all he said.
With hoe in hand,
Around the corn, alfalfa and the sugar beets
We walked the farmer's walk.

Eyes on the crops,
Slow methodical stutter steps we took.
Through one field, into another,
We walked away the acres,
Warmed by the summer sun.

Papá never talked—
A waste of time?
Nothing to say?
I learned it was his way.
It didn't matter,
I listened and watched
His every movement,
From the corners of my eyes,
Afraid to ask a child's question—why?

He was short by grown men's measure,
But thick muscled and bull strong,

With a confident, graceful walk,
Like a dancer, he wasted little motion
When he walked the farmer's walk.

He wore his farmer's hat
To shield his small, clear,
Beady, penetrating eyes.
He saw all,
Missed nothing.
I feared those eagle eyes and always
Avoided their gaze.
They saw through everything.
They were judging eyes,
Never seeing good,
Or innocence.
Everything was poor
And found wanting—through those eyes.
But still, more fear, than love or respect—I had,
And so I followed him,
When he called on those warm summer days.
I came running, didn't delay
From wherever he did bay,
For me to take beside him
And walk—.

The farmer's walk.

I See Your Face

I walk
In fields of brown,
Once trod by weathered boots
With labored strides,
Warmed by a summer sun
From a different time.
I close my eyes.
I'm there again.
I feel your spirit,
Fresh on migrant mornings.

I'm filled with wonder,
That once we lived
In a world where light
Filled our eyes,
Our nights were inhabited
By the magic of our dreams,
And angels kept watch
And held tight our
Vulnerable souls.

Dark dissipates
And the sun evaporates
The crystal dew
That lies delicately
On the mint leaves
Growing in the fields.

I walk—
Each step disturbs the dirt
And in the dust
That blooms,
A thought, a word
Or a vision is reborn
To delicately die
In the dust that settles
Behind me.

The sun casts shadows
That echo through
The empty house
We abandoned
When we were young,
And you were strong.

Dirty windows of time diffuse
Vivid images
Of empty rooms
With walls that mysteriously
Echo the innocence of childhood dreams
In salty tears and words,
Now peeling with the paint.

It was, I recall
A hot day in July
When you ran,
Escaped...
With your precious brood;
Nine of us in tow,
Across the valley of
Vineyards and orchards
Into safety.

I feel your breath
On my skin
In the sweet, fragrant
Breeze that blows
Through the peach trees.

I feel it elegantly, gracefully
Caress my brow
As I place
Each ripe peach
Carefully in the wooden
Boxes I fill and take
To the Saturday Market.

Sometimes I awake
To feel your hand lightly
Graze mine and I wonder
Where you are
And how it is
I still feel you
On my skin
After all these years
Of dusty miles.

Your wrinkled hand
Now worn, but still warm,
Like a delicate piece
Of fine leather,
Taut, now opaque
Stretched over brittle, gnarled bones no longer
Strong.

I look into your eyes
No longer youthfully bright,
Now blurry with age
And wonder what they saw,
When the world was new
And you were young.
You were beautiful then,
I know—
I've seen the Kodak black and whites,
That guard the wall
In the hall.

Lovers have come and gone
But your children follow you
And gather still—around you like
A mother hen's
Chirping, yellow chicks.

I see your ailing body
Bent and broken by
Years of hard labor
And I wonder
If it is me I'm seeing,
And it frightens me.

Still I see the dignity
And beauty,
The strength
And vitality
That once
Gave birth to me,
And many others,
And the future frightens me
Because your passing lies there,
Somewhere in the cold
Of an unknown wilderness.

I spent youthful years
Running from you,
And I'll spend the rest—what's left
Searching,
And you will be gone,
And that frightens me.

Mamá, your passing
Frightens me so.

I see your face.

Strawberry Fields And Airplanes

I was seven when it happened. I was sitting in the middle of a strawberry field as only a seven-year-old could: mouth full of strawberries and sticky red juice trickling down my chin, staining my faded Davy Crockett T-shirt. It had been a shirt worn and outgrown by two older brothers. It had a few holes, but was none worse for a little wear. If I was careful, my younger brother Mario would inherit it soon.

I was supposed to be hard at work, picking the berries, not basking in the warmth and beauty of the day. Like countless laborers before me, stretching back in an unbroken line two hundred years—or two thousand—I was there to work, not daydream. And in my child's mind, the beauty of the day was no salve for the sting of a hard day's labor. But as I looked out over the acres of strawberry fields set to the backdrop of the fir trees and jagged, white Cascade Mountains, I couldn't help but feel my heart lift. And then … it happened: a small thing, really, but one that would change my life forever.

We had woken to a cool summer morning, my brothers and I. The fire, long since burned out, was cold gray ash. We had shivered, dressing quickly, quietly. It was cold. And with the prospect of a long day in the fields looming over us, we hadn't been in the mood for good-natured kidding. Hands in our pockets, we'd walked single file to Mamá's cabin through a camp shrouded in a gentle fog that obscured the bottoms of the cabins. The rickety wooden structures appeared to float in a churning sea of gray-white.

Though of course I didn't think anything of it at the time, the world we lived in was as crude, raw and simple as what laborers lived in two hundred years earlier. It was an unencumbered, dangerous life of a nomadic agricultural worker. The fact four of my older siblings had met untimely deaths in childhood was proof it could be brutal. Later, I heard it described as romantic, but as a child I saw no romance in it. And in retrospect, I see little that could be so construed.

From year to year we followed the seasonal crops from state to state, from one agricultural community to another. We had no transportation. We relied on the benevolence of friends and traveled on the back of a flatbed half-ton truck, which a hundred years before would have been a horse-drawn wagon, and a hundred years before that, would have meant pack animals. It was faster, but probably not as clean: when it wasn't being used to transport migrants, it was transporting cattle. It reeked.

By the time we had finished breakfast and walked to the south field, the fog had begun to dissipate, retreating silently into the wet woods. The sun had been flashing over the fir trees in the east as the dew evaporated from the strawberry leaves. We'd methodically picked up one row and down another all morning, as the sun had grown warmer on our backs. Mamá, about twenty feet ahead of us, had finished her row, stood up, and stretched her aching back. Seeing we were right behind her, she'd told us to meet her under the canopy of fir boughs at the end of the field when we'd finished our rows.

When we'd first arrived, she'd placed a tub of bean burritos wrapped in white cotton dish rags in the shade of the firs, accurately projecting where we would be when the sun was overhead. As we'd finished, we'd gathered around her and waited for freshly made burritos. We'd eaten with quiet relish as she talked to us about the day: how long it would take to finish this field and which one we would be in tomorrow. When we'd finished with one, she'd handed us each another and then another until the tub was empty and our hunger satiated. We'd drunk water from a glass gallon jug she'd half buried alongside the tub that contained our lunch.

Looking back on those wonderful lunches, eaten with strawberry-stained hands and dirt under our fingernails, I wonder how she always knew exactly how many burritos to make. When lunch ended, there was never one too few or too many. And no one ever complained they didn't get enough. Each morning when she woke to prepare our breakfast and pack our lunch, how did she match the number of burritos to the day's appetites? Or did we simply adjust our appetites to what she packed?

After our repast, the afternoon had begun where the morning left off, except for an unexpected light misting that came and went on the hour. It was in a sunny period that it happened: that's when I saw the airplane.

Strawberry-stained, fully engaged in a post-lunch daydream, I was supposed to be picking when I heard a faint rumble up among the clouds. I looked up - and was mesmerized by the arc of an airplane with a long, white vapor tail. I tracked it as it slowly dwindled toward the vast horizon, above the tips of the high wall of old fir trees.

I sat awed. Man. Flying. Strange as it seems to me today, I don't recall having thought before of humans flying; nor could I grasp the kind of magic it took to make that happen. "Only birds can fly," I heard myself whisper.

As the sky beyond the trees swallowed the plane up, I wondered if I'd really seen it. Was it a figment of my overactive imagination? And what was that long white tail about? I couldn't have imagined such a tail. Wonderment flooded my senses.

The meaning of what I had seen hit me like a thunderclap. I began to struggle with what I sensed to be a conflict in realities. The airplane—man flying—became an emblem of a newly discovered world unfolding before my mind's eye. Here I was, fully engaged in this primitive lifestyle—specifically, sitting in the cool dirt in the middle of a strawberry field and, more generally, living in a labor camp that could have easily been mistaken by ethnographers as an encampment from two hundred years ago. The contrast was suddenly startling, morphing from the airplane into a whole world teeming with possibilities. The airplane birthed into existence a future I had had no idea existed until that moment. And with it was born my conscious desire to be part of it.

I had never before recognized the primitive quality of my life. We owned nothing more than what we could carry on our backs. We had no home, no washer or dryer, no beds or dresser drawers. We didn't have need of a bank account, for we lived hand to mouth. We didn't have a dollar to spare, nor did we accumulate any in our pockets. We paid no taxes, nor did we know they were due. Doctors, lawyers, hospitals, or health plans were out of our reach, if not understanding. If we experienced problems, needs or wants, whatever they might have been, we provided for them with the meager resources we had immediately at our disposal. When we became ill, we understood our two choices: one worse than the other and neither of them good. We could go to the hospital, place our sick loved ones on the Anglos' altars of healing and plead with the white gods in heavily starched white frocks for their benevolence.

On two occasions we did that—and our young died for want of treatment. My padres were never quite sure what they died from, but they were sure they could have been saved had they been treated. The second choice was to use whatever folk medicine was available within our community, pray, watch, and wait. Two died as we prayed, watched, and waited. We buried four in obscure places long forgotten and since there were more to care for, went to sleep with the heavy burden of a child's death on our hearts. When we woke the next morning, the fields were waiting for us, and we moved on to the next one as best we could. Papá has gone home to meet them and Mamá still dreams of them in the stillness and quiet of her lonely nights. And still, she wonders why it had to be that way.

Our education consisted of cultural myths and folklore handed down in the oral tradition from generation to generation, and what little we gleaned from our hit-and-miss public school education between harvest seasons. We lived in dilapidated, rat-infested, one-room wooden shacks with woodstoves for heating and cooking. There were no indoor bathrooms, plumbing, or running water; no rent or damage deposit was necessary. In the summer you fought the incessant bugs and vile rodents for ownership, and since possession was nine-tenths of the law, ownership switched hands often. In the winter the wind blew freely through the warped walls and up through the cracks in floorboards, leaving us at the mercy of a stoked woodstove and the memory of one of us to feed it in the waning hours of a freezing night or morning.

We cultivated the peripheral edge of modern America. We roamed the countryside, working the fields and picking the crops that automation had yet to touch, doing the work Anglo citizenry had grown too affluent to see the work as honorable or worthy of their effort. We worked on the fringe and watched with curious fascination a world we had little working knowledge of, and whose occupants deemed us invisible.

As I sat in the rich, brown loam, watching the happenings outside and feeling the changes within, our eighteenth-century existence collided with a flying man of the twentieth century and, in a crescendo of emotions, ignited in me a passion to reconcile one against the other. As I thought about it, I shuddered, as if touched by a jolt of electricity. I looked around to see if anyone around me had noticed the physical spasm my body must have made. No one seemed to. Now that I saw it and felt it, I longed for a closer examination. I wanted to explore the intricacies, feel the textures, and more importantly, understand this new world I assumed had been unavailable to a Mexican, migrant worker with no credentials for membership or belonging. But I desperately wanted to become a part of this world, without having the first idea how, or knowing if it were even possible.

It was one thing to acknowledge the world around me, and altogether something different to understand how to circumnavigate it. But, despite my young age, I innately understood my future, my survival, was inextricably linked to, dependent on finding my way through the morass of this other culture.

There was no one to guide me. No one to help me make the critical decisions necessary to successfully enter and navigate the modern world. I couldn't consult my older siblings. They were caught up in their own struggles of survival and would not have wanted to be bothered with mine.

Somehow I finished the day's work. At the end of it, lying on my top bunk, I sensed what had to be done. I solemnly concluded I needed to abandon one culture to embrace the other. I pledged to rid myself of as much of my Mexican culture as humanly possible. And every day thereafter, like peeling an onion, I slowly and consciously began to abandon and close the door on my native culture.

What I couldn't have known or guessed were the sacrifices that would need to be made, by me and, inadvertently, my family as well. Every step forward, I learned, had three parts to it; the learning that needed to be embraced, the part of my culture needing to be unlearned—and the inevitable sacrifices that accompanied the process.

It began with language. One of the obvious differences standing between the Anglos and us Mexicans was language. If we spoke English it was with a thick accent. The accent identified you as being different and brought attention and ridicule. I vowed to get rid of the accent and speak English as perfectly as the Anglos. In an effort to accomplish that, I decided I would no longer speak Spanish, to anyone; family or friends. Considering everyone we lived with and around spoke Spanish, it was not an easy proposition. The sacrifice was the loss of friends and respect within our Mexican community. I persisted. I know it must have infuriated, and certainly embarrassed my mother. To have a child who would not converse with her in Spanish must have been difficult. Only a few times, exasperated by my insolence, did she show any anger or impatience with me. Most of the time her response was the unreadable, Mona Lisa, enigmatic smile.

Mamá, a profoundly intuitive person, somehow understood what I was going through and patiently but reluctantly made the necessary adjustments to accommodate me. One of her adjustments was to try and learn more English. It was a slow and difficult process. And she had her Mexican pride to contend with. She would not try out words until she was sure she not only understood them, but could say them with some articulation. She would not be laughed at by anyone.

Today when we get together, out of respect, I attempt to converse in Spanish with her. When I do so she impatiently waves her hand, telling me to stop. We both laugh but understand the uncomfortable truth we've settled into. She knows enough English to understand me and I know enough Spanish to understand her. But that I've abandoned our culture to embrace another is not lost on her. If she judges me harshly, she's never said. That's not been the case with some of my siblings. My actions have not always been met with their approval and to this day, their dismay, on occasion can be heard in an errant comment or observed in a raised eyebrow.

The repercussions of leaving the sanctity, safety, and innocence of my origins would not be felt nor fully understood until it was too late to return. Once initiated, the experience took a life of its own. It took a nanosecond to be aware of the strange, fascinating, and unique situation in which I found myself, that warm July afternoon in the middle of a strawberry field, but I will spend the rest of my life reconciling a decision made as an innocent, ignorant child.

No longer being willing to speak Spanish was not the only way I abandoned my native culture, although it was the most egregious. As I closed that door, I quietly opened and embraced the other. In the end, as I sit here writing this account, I'm struck by what I've learned about my beginnings and the journey to enlightenment. You can't abandon a culture without feeling an intimate loss so great it leaves you forever searching for your home and true identity.

I Meant to Ask You

I meant to ask you about your childhood;
When your parents died,
First your Mamá and then your Papá.
You were abandoned to the streets,
With no one to feed or clothe you.
With no one to protect you.
Were you afraid?
How did you survive?
Is that what made you a hard man?

I meant to ask you about Montana;
The miserable winter cold,
The sweltering summer heat,
Working in the fields,
From sun-up to sun-down.
What was it like for you,
On your own,
All alone?

I meant to ask you about meeting Mamá.
About the sugar beet fields,
And living in migrant labor camps.
I remember the Kodak black and white
Of both of you.
She was so beautiful
And you so handsome.
Did you love her?

I meant to ask you about the children;
Sixteen give or take a brown baby.
Did you mean to have a large family,
Or was that Mamá's idea?
Did you want us all,
Or were we a burden?
We never knew.

I meant to ask you about Mamá.
Why you never married her.
Not that she complained.
She loved you so.
Even now—
After all the years
Tears still run down her cheeks when she looks
At your handsome face
Staring at her from the wall.

I meant to ask you about Manuel and Chavelo.
First Manuel, then Chavelo
Left home and never returned.
They joined the Air Force
Without your permission.
Did you realize
It was the beginning of the end
Of your family?

I meant to ask you about Mamá leaving.
Did it break your heart when she left,
With nine of us in tow,
And married George—a gringo?
Did you feel devastated like I felt
When Cathy left me with our children,
To marry another man—a gringo?
Did your heart ever heal?
Mine never has.

I meant to ask you about George.
How did it feel when you learned he
Was twice the father you ever were,
And that we grew to love him?
Did it hurt you?
It felt wonderful to feel

A father's love for the first time
At age eleven,
But terrible knowing it should
Have been your love.
I still feel the pain.
Does it ever go away?

I meant to ask you about the storms.
About what to do when
The rain, thunder and wind
Made the house shudder and shake,
And washed my confidence away.
Storms still scare me.

I meant to ask you about white people.
What should I have done when the insensitive people
Called me names because they didn't
Like the color of my skin.
Even yet, the echoes of their cruel abuse
Leaves me mute with fear.

I meant to ask you about the war.
When I was drafted
I didn't know what to do;
To participate in an unjust war,
Protest and go to jail
Or hide in Canada.
I went to war,
But still I feel the coward
Because I should have protested,
Not fought.
Only later did I find
The hero isn't always
The one who goes to fight,
Or the one who comes home dismembered,
Or crazy,
Or the one who comes home in a box.

I meant to ask you about life,
If sometimes you weren't sure about it,
If you were ever so discouraged
You wanted to give up,
Like I do sometimes,
When I wake up in blackness
So dark and consumed in pain so deep
I can only think
Of making it stop,
To make it feel better?

I meant to ask you about parenting.
How did it feel when you whipped me
With your belt when I was too
Young to understand why.
Did you feel as badly as I did
When I hit my son
When he too was too
Young to understand why?

I meant to ask you about God.
What to do when I feel He's abandoned me.
When my prayers go unanswered
And I feel so incredibly alone.
The night is darkest inside a soul
That has reached out to God
Only to hear nothing—and feel nothing,
But the beating of his own heart.
I often wish for Him to wrap me in His glory,
But sometimes I can't find Him,
No matter how I try.
No matter how I cry.
Was it the same for you sometimes?

I meant to ask you about us.
How it felt when all your children
Abandoned you.
You wanted us to run the farm
And take care of you in your old age,
But none of us listened.
None of us would help you.
How did it feel?
Did you hold a grudge?
Did you curse us?
Did you hate us?

I meant to ask you about your last day.
What you wanted from me when
I came to your hospital room
In the middle of the night.
I knew you were dying.
I found you lingering between
Earth and a place beyond;
Between the pain killers
And the hopelessness of the
Reality that you were trying
To hold on to.
Your eyes were glassy
Your tongue dry
But still I thought of myself.
I desperately wanted to hear
You say you loved me.
At least once I wanted to hear it,
Before you passed on,
But you never said it,
And neither did I.
It's always been easier to hate you—old man
But at least once
I wished I could have told you the truth;
I loved you.
I'm sorry I never told you.
And disappointed I never heard it.

I meant to ask you about growing old.
What I'm supposed to do when
I get too old and weak to fight anymore,
Too blind to see tomorrow,
Too lame to walk away,
What to do when my children
Leave me and I long to recline
Within the safety of their love.
To be embraced.
To be touched.
Did you feel the same way,
In your last days?

I meant to ask you if you were afraid I'd become like you?
If you wished me to turn out differently;
To be more sensitive and kind,
To love my family more,
And not be afraid to tell them
How much they meant to me.
I have always been afraid I would
Turn out like you,
But all along I knew I would.
I fought it for years.
I wished I'd told you
I'd lost the fight.
I am you.

I meant to ask you
What you thought of me.
Did you ever wonder what
I thought of you?

I meant to ask you—Papá.

As A Child

As a child—
I sat beside the irrigation ditch;
The house above,
And fields below,
And on those hot summer days
When the irrigation water gate was opened
I watched the cool water flow.

As a child—
I sat beside the irrigation ditch
And sailed my wooden boat
(The one Juan made for me),
Through green alfalfa fields
And rows of yellow corn,
Whose stalks waved to the clouds,
As I floated bravely by.

With billowed sails,
And rudder strong,
I sailed to shores far and wide.
I found adventures
In foreign lands,
And fought in battles
On sea and sand.

I sailed the Great Lakes:
Superior, Michigan, Huron, Erie and Ontario.
I sailed down the great river Nile.
I sailed far and away
Being sailor brave
Always strong, I never swayed.

I sailed down the muddy Mississippi
To the Gulf of Mexico,
And into the great Atlantic.
I was courageous but careful
And never once,
No, I never panicked.

I sailed on the Euphrates
Past Baghdad and Babylon
That flowed into the Persian Gulf.
The trip was long and tough.

And when the big orange sun
Was low and sinking behind
The Horse Heaven Hills of home,
I heard Mama calling
To come to dinner.
It was time to sail home.

And on the trusty, sturdy sailboat
That Juan made for me,
On those warm summer evenings
Of my youth,
I sailed the seven seas.

As a child.

And I Will Give You

I saw you looking, Mamá,
Wistfully.
You reached the end of the row
And stopped—momentarily.
You stood up,
And looked aside.
What were you searching for?
Was it something or someone?

What was on your mind,
In your eye,
The life ahead,
Or a child behind?
A sudden glimpse of one that's gone?
He was close by, following along.
She was sitting over there—
In a chair.
They were playing in the brown dirt,
Beneath the gnarled willow tree
That stood gallantly,
Courageously among the broken
Wooden shacks of the migrant camp,
We lived in for a season.

You couldn't think about it,
Could you?
A heart never heals when a child's
Death breaks it,
Does it?
So much lost, too soon.
And every day is another day,
Another way
For a wounded heart to bleed.
But you had to move along, didn't you,
In the hot migrant sun?
The rows were waiting for you,
And the rest of your brood too.

And I will give you castles in the sky,
With diamonds and pearls to beautify.
And on those warm summer days
I will give you the cool evening breeze
In fields of golden wheat
Where you can flutter in the sky
With the pretty monarch butterflies.

But still, did you wonder,
How a mamá was supposed to do it—heal, that is,
When her diamonds are spewed and lost in the dirt?
Marta, who could have been a queen,
And Mario, he might have been a Dean.

God gives so little to the poor,
That when the miracle children are born,
It matters naught that you will never have
Anything but your children.
And they become your diamonds in the sun.
And for you—they sparkle and shine,
Like the hope they give you
And you give them.
The hope of something better.
And, isn't it Mamá, that hope that slowly began to die?
I could see it in your eyes.

I saw you looking, Mamá.
At the end of the day,
Chores were done,
Children were bathed and sleeping;
Dreaming dreams that children dream,
Playing house or submarines.
You were sipping coffee—cream and sugar,
I remember.
You were looking out the kitchen window,
Rooster crowing at the setting sun,
Day was hard, but now was done.

And it was then I heard a sigh,
A deep and lonely one,
And it made me wonder why.
Was the future playing in your mind,
Stately mansions by and by?
Or did you see us grown and gone
Successful, rich or thereupon?
Or were you simply wondering when
Life would get easier—then again,
Hope can be a child's playpen.
And for you, just surviving another day
Seemed a cold, malevolent cliché.

And I will give you castles in the sky,
With diamonds and pearls to beautify.
And on those warm summer days
I will give you the cool evening breeze
In fields of golden wheat
Where you can flutter in the sky
With the pretty monarch butterflies.

I saw you looking, Mamá.
We were traveling on the back
Of a flatbed motor-truck.
Your arms were wrapped around your legs.
Your chin rested on your knees,
As we rode beneath a canvas canopy.
The wind was playing with your hair,
And fluffy clouds were cotton prayers.
We were eating bologna sandwiches,
And it was then that I saw
You brush some hair away from your mouth,
And then you quietly closed your eyes
And slipped into your world of dreams.

Was it of a farm of our own,
With cows in pastures green,
Surrounded by hills serene,
And horses to ride and big red barns
With white fences that ran straight like lines?
Did it have acres of garden that you love,
With watermelons and cantaloupe,
Corn, green beans and green jalapeño peppers?
And flowers everywhere—yes, the flowers.
I knew you loved your flowers so.
Everywhere we landed, you made them grow.

I don't know, but let me ask,
In a poor woman's mind,
Does one dare to dream so bold,
And wish so deep?
Is not hope a dangerous thing,
And a wish a careless fling?

And I will give you castles in the sky,
With diamonds and pearls to beautify.
And on those warm summer days
I will give you the cool evening breeze
In fields of golden wheat
Where you can flutter in the sky
With the pretty monarch butterflies.

I saw you looking, Mamá.

My Way Back

Quite and solitary,
I often sit,
In Italian leather chair
Overlooking pastures green,
Horses and farm houses serene.

Often it makes me wonder,
When times are quiet,
Why four cold bodies lie
In lonely graveyard hill,
While I live in bucolic country still.

I survived when others didn't.
Did their luck run out?
And then they went,
Were their tiny souls
Heaven sent?

What was the path,
From whence I came,
The one took through,
A life reclaimed?

Of those migrant years,
I have no shame,
But not be said,
The same of fears
But not be said
The same of tears.

From the soil I came,
From somewhere hence;
To the soil I go in recompense.

What was the road I did travel,
Was it asphalt, dirt or gravel?
The road was hard in getting there.
Will leaving be a different fare?

Was it something Mamá said,
When fantasies were in her head,
Or the hardness of Papá's labor,
A difference he might favor.

The reason, it is important,
The way it happened,
The route I took,
So you can read this
Sometime hence,
And know you too
Can jump the fence.

It's not easy,
But I might say,
It's about the hope,
That Mamá gave,
And hard work too.
That Papá knew.

And maybe therein
Lies the answer.
Maybe it's the way
For you to know,
That in hopes,
And hard work,
Is found the doorway,
Down the hall and
Through the hallway.

I pray my ashes to be spread,
By those I've loved,
For whom I've bled,
On migrant fields,
To nurture soil,
Increase the yield,
For the next generation,
Can be revealed.

From the soil I came,
From somewhere hence,
To the soil I go in recompense.

My way back.

Mamá When...

Mamá,
When I went to war
Did you wonder why I had to go?
I knew you'd been there before:
Four and one for sure.
How did it feel?
Was it the same then again,
When I walked out the door?

And when the sun came
Tumbling down,
Did you wonder if I would
Again ever be around?
And as you slept that night
Was I in your dreams?
Did you toss and turn?
Did you get up to check
The night light on the stove
To see if it had gone out?

Did you wake up in the morning
And wonder if it was true?
Did you pinch yourself?
What else could you do?
And as you gazed sleepily
Out morning window
While drinking your coffee,
Were any thoughts of me?

And it was give or take
A brown boy.
Four had gone before.
Two more waiting
On the shore.
Two more waiting
To be shorn.

Mamá when I returned—alive
But, so unwell.
Did you rejoice
It wasn't in a body-bag?
And did you cry
As you made me beans and rice?
You touched my hand
So tenderly when you handed
Me a tortilla

I did.
I hoped you hadn't seen
My tears when they dropped
From my cheeks
And mixed
With the beans and rice,
I thought I would never
Taste again.

Mamá when you look at me,
Do you think
Your children will someday see
A country that will ever be
For her, him and me:
Immigrants all, longing to be free?

And Mamá now that
Papá's dead and gone
Do you miss him
In the night?
Do you still think
What you did was right?
In leaving,
And giving up the fight?

Mamá when you're gone
I'm going to wish
It will not be for long.
I'm going to rise each morning
And look for you
Among the flowers in the garden,
Kendra plants for you.
And when I retire each evening
And lay my head on pillows soft,
I will search for you in my dreams.

Mamá when you see me in heaven
Will I be number five, six or seven?"
And will I still be yours
And will you still be mine?

And it was give or take
A brown boy.
Four had gone before.
Two more waiting
On the shore.
Two more waiting
To be shorn.

Mamá when…

But, I'm Not Mexican Anymore

When I was six, I went to school.
All the children were happy.
I stood clutching sister Raquel's hand
And listening to the chatter all around me.
Worried—I looked up and said,
"No entiendo nada!"
What was I to do?
She smiled, patted me on the head
And walked out of the door.
I lost her in a blur of tears
And confusion

But, I'm not Mexican anymore.

When we sat down to eat
I pulled out two burritos
Wrapped in wax paper,
From a used brown paper bag.
Two children around me whispered,
Pointed and laughed.
"What is he eating," One asked?

But, I'm not Mexican anymore.

Later in the third grade we
Had a vocabulary test
I didn't understand the words
But was intuitive and
Matched them
With their meanings—as best I could.
I got eight out of ten
And was proud.

But I'm not Mexican anymore.

Every time I spoke the children giggled.
The teacher shook her head and corrected me,
And they looked at me with pity.
Dirty brown kid—I knew they scorned.

But, I'm not Mexican anymore.

Every night I spent time in the bathroom
Pronouncing the vocabulary words
In front of the only mirror in the house;
Practicing moving my lips and tongue
Like they did—the white kids.

But I'm not Mexican anymore.

I wouldn't speak Spanish
To my parents anymore.
But they understood.
They didn't ridicule.
They knew what I was doing.
They knew how I was suffering.

But I'm not Mexican anymore.

In seventh grade—P.E. class
Playing basketball in the gym
Wearing Pat Millers sweatshirt
When I heard Coach Miller
Say to his son,
"Why is that dirty Mexican
Wearing your sweatshirt?"
Get it back,
But don't put it on.
Your mom will wash it first.

But, I'm not Mexican anymore.

In high school, Carlos Cruz and I
Sat in the back—no other seats.
No books for us to read.
Our names were never called
For roll that day—or any day.
We didn't exist.
I looked at him
And he at me.
What did it matter
That we were free?

But, I'm not Mexican anymore.

In Guam, flying into Vietnam,
Miguel Sanchez said to me,
"Ramon, you must be Mexican?
And I said, yes, I mean sí,
I am."
And he looked at me...
And shook his head,
Back home my Mexican friends
Would slit your throat
For talking like that.

But, I'm not Mexican anymore.

And here I am,
A man sad of many years
Who wants to be,
What once he was.

But, I'm not Mexican anymore.

Biography

Ramón Mesa Ledesma was born in Toppenish, Washington, into a family of sixteen brothers and sisters. He spent his formative years in migrant labor camps throughout the Pacific Northwest. He attended Mount Vernon High School through his junior year and graduated from Glenwood High School in Glenwood, Washington in 1966. After graduation he joined the Air Force and was a crew chief on a KC-135A, flying refueling missions over Vietnam. During the Vietnam War he was stationed at Fairchild Air Force, near Spokane, Washington and flew out of bases in Thailand, Okinawa and Guam. After Vietnam he attended Spokane Falls Community College and Eastern Washington State College, now Eastern Washington University, earning a BA and M.Ed. As an undergraduate he studied history, sociology, and anthropology. His graduate studies were in counseling.

Ramón lives with his wife, Kendra, a high school mathematics teacher, three dogs, a cat, and an assortment of bear, coyotes, rabbits, and deer on ten acres in rural Sedro Woolley, Washington. He splits his time between a private family counseling practice in Stanwood and writing children's books, poetry and short stories.

Special Thanks

I would like to thank James Bertolino, a great poet, for helping me edit this work. His advice has been invaluable to me.

I'd also like to thank Ruben Carrera for helping me with the Spanish words scattered throughout this work.

And thanks to Charles Jones, a friend and long time mentor. His wonderful poetry inspired me to write my own.

Cover Art Work

Book cover art was painted by Jess Arashi Hara. Jess was born in Moses Lake, Washington and raised in Bellingham, Washington. She studied art at Cornish College of the Arts in Seattle and graduated with a BFA. In their previous collaboration, Ms. Hara provided the illustrations for Ramón's children's book, *Tomás And The Magic Race Cars*.

CPSIA information can be obtained
at www.ICGtesting.com
Printed in the USA
BVHW012046090322
630905BV00014B/133